Daydreaming Poetry

Iris Carden

Published by: Iris Carden
            Ipswich, Qld, Australia
            iriscardenauthor.net

ISBN: 978-0-6459679-2-0

Cover Art: Windmill by Iris Carden

A catalogue record for this work is available from the National Library of Australia

Contents

Teach Your Daughter

Teach your daughter all she can achieve.
The world will teach her all that she can't.
Help her to know, and to believe,
What she can do when she follows her heart.

Teach your daughter her links to the Earth
the ground she walks on which provides her food.
Teach her the value of water, soil and air,
things that are clean and true and good.

Teach her about her links to Heaven and hope.
The world will teacher her fear, loss and despair.
Teach her things matter beyond just today.
Teach her of love, joy, compassion and care.

Each year, as she grows, and learns more and more.
Bring out the best from your knowledge-store.
The world will try to fit her to a mould,
Teach her she's always free to be more.

Show her the path that you have walked,
Where you were right and where you were wrong.
Then stand back to let he walk her on own,
She will go so much further than you have gone.

Writing a Poem

You can write a poem
give it structure and rhyme
but maybe you don't want to
so you don't.

You can give it a rhythm
that rolls off the tongue,
that makes the words feel
like they should be sung.

Or you can
abandon structure,
rhythm, and rhyme,
and let your mind just go
chasing a random idea.
Then you write a
rambling,
ambling,
occasionally scrambling,
mindlessly meandering,
unguided,
unplanned,
totally out of hand,
getting harder to understand,
undirected,
disconnected,
oh there's a cat,
stream-of-consciousness vomit.

You can distill wisdom into
short and simple words.
You can obfuscate stupidity
with grandiloquent, obscure terms.

You can bend language
like a prism bends the light.
You can inspire dreams,
give imagination flight.

The poet has the power
of words and where they go.
But if it's any good,
only the reader knows.

Grace

She maintains an air
of subtle, gentle, grace.
No matter the event
no matter what the pace.

Nothing ever seems
to interrupt her calm
even if others panic,
even if there's an alarm.

She glides through life
with poise and with elegance.
She never does a thing
to cause someone offence.

She's admired by those
who think their life is a mess.
They wish that they had been
with such grace and poise blessed.

She gets things done always
in the most efficient way.
And somehow finds the time
to help others through the day.

But no-one sees the work
behind the calm facade.
To stay poised and elegant
takes working very hard.

No-one knows her struggles
while she seems so calm and strong.
But deep below the surface,
she fights battles of her own.

She doesn't share her troubles
with those who share her life.
She would never burden
others with any of her strife.

And if you feel inadequate
with all you see her do,
just know, below the surface,
she feels the same way too.

Shelter

Who will be your shelter
in the storms of life?
Who will protect you
from toil and strife?

Who will keep you safe,
and guard you from all harm?
Who will be your anchor
in times of alarm?

Have you learned the secret?
Have you heard the word.
How to keep safe
in a troubling world?

Become your own shelter
for all the storms of life.
Protect yourself from danger,
from all the toil and strife.

Friendship and even love
should be given free.
Not something dependent
on insecurity and need.

Perhaps you'll find someone
who will face the storms with you.
But with them, or alone,
you will make it through.

After the Storm

Winds growing strong.
Clouds gather dark.
The tumult begins.
Storm of the heart.

Sky tears begin,
'mid howling shrieks.
Bend now or break.
Resistance is weak

After the storm,
peaceful garden.
Jewelled tear drops.
Flowers glisten.

Pain is exhausted.
Emotion at rest.
Glistening garden.
Shining its best.

Words Fail Me

Hey!
Do you want to go to…
ahhhh the place…
You know, the place where…
Arrrrrrk!
The place where you….
Ahhhhh!
The place where you do the thing….
You know the thing…
The thingy thing….
The place where you do the thingy thing…
The PLACE where you do the thingy THIIIIIIING!
Brain malfunction
Error code 404: Words not found.

Somewhere

Somewhere the road crosses over the rainbow,
Somewhere the phoenix sings,
Somewhere a volcano erupts a chocolate flow.
Perhaps it's a story. Perhaps it's a dream.

Somewhere all people have enough to eat,
Somewhere everyone has a home,
Somewhere everyone's equal.
Perhaps it's a story. Perhaps it's a dream.

Housework

They say nothing lasts for ever,
but that's not really true.
There's always dirty dishes,
and dirty laundry too.

You think it's all caught up,
and your home looks fine.
Then domestic demons laugh,
at the mess you later find.

So you sweep and dust.
Oh that familiar refrain!
Then you mop and wash,
and go back to the start again.

The work will never end.
Domestic labour's a kind of hell.
As everyone who's done it,
knows only far too well.

Words

Sometimes I get to the end of the day,
and I haven't written anything,
the words just haven't come.
I don't know where they went,
but they didn't visit me.
I get tired, and impatient,
with those annoying words.
But the words don't care.
They taunt me from a distance,
as I give up and
f
 a
  l
  l
   a   s   l   e   e   e   e

17

The Writer's Friend

For weird, arcane, information,
Google search is the writer's friend,
I search for the strangest things,
sometimes now and then.

I've asked what would happen,
should space junk start to fall,
and just how much junk
is orbiting us, after all?

I've asked about Rasputin's
life, and his family tree.
If he had relatives,
where would they be?

What would happen to a gun
if the barrel were blocked?
Would it explode?
Would that give you a shock?

How deep should you bury
a corpse under the roses,
so the smell won't alert
your neighbours' noses?

And what can you grow
in natural Martian soil?
What reward would there be
for a gardener's toil?

I'd need to spend so much
research time in the library,
if Google search
weren't available, free.

Grocery List

I'm making a list, checking it twice.
Do I need coffee? Do I need rice?
Is there something I could live without?
Saving some money's what it's all about.
The news calls it a "cost of living crisis."
Don't overspend on seasonings and spices.
Has yoghurt become a luxury now?
Could I cut out more things somehow?
Can I cut a few dollars here or there?
Can I save any money anywhere?

At least, I'm lucky, a roof over my head.
Too many don't have rent money to spend.
For some people it's just an adjustment or two,
For others, there's no paying the bills that are due.
Inflation is rising, corporate profits soar,
a nightmare for middle-income, and poor.
Governments could act, if they had the will,
but campaigns depend on donations, still.

Could the system be made a little more fair
by taxing corporations and millionaires?
Instead of tax breaks, for obscene wealth,
ensure for everyone: home, food and health.
But the system is broken, and everyone knows:
the wealthy grow richer, while poverty grows.
So if your personal cost of life's in crisis,
remember someone's getting richer from this.

If you're struggling, it's time to get mad,
see your local politician, and make them sad.
Give them a challenge. Give them a choice.
Tell them you'll make your vote your voice.
"Cost of living" is not just a set of buzz words,
not when it's a cost some can't afford.
Playing with human lives isn't a fair game,
you can't make it fairer, by not knowing their names.

And if like me, you've got a safe roof,
and a few tweaks of the list still give enough food,
remember that others have it way worse.
This "cost of living crisis" is a national curse.
You can call me a socialist, I just don't care,
I just want to live in a country that's fair.
No-one deserves to live on the street.
No-one deserves to have nothing to eat.

An Act of Spidercide

When I saw you sitting on the wall, I said, "Hi," and moved on,
knowing how you helped protect my pest-free home.
I thought we had an understanding, our intentions were allied,
I never wanted to commit a cruel act of spidercide.

Instead, my friend, you chose a strange place to hide.
BecauseI didn't think to look, that's why I never spied.
I only went to pour myself a glass of soda water,
not thinking that you would be where you never ought to.

I never thought that I would see you floating to the top,
I jumped when I saw you, and of course my pouring stopped.
Had I been able to see your very tiny eyes,
would I have seen them show shock, betrayal, or surprise?

You scrambled out of the liquid, onto the side of the cup.
While I grabbed a paper towel, and cleaned my spilled water
up.
You sat on the outside of the glass, and I left you there to dry.
I left you to yourself, and I thought you would be fine.

I tried not to upset you more, leaving the glass on the table.
I thought you'd dry out and then move on when you felt able.
I went about my day, not thinking about you any further,
not imagining a simple drink, would lead to spider murder.

I can't imagine what possessed you to make your next move.
Did you think that sofa water was something you might love?
Once you were safely out, why did you go back in?
Was leaving you like that, such a terrible sin?

When I came back later, I'll admit I was disturbed,
To find you floating dead, your legs all tightly curled
Have I learned a lesson from this gruesomeness near past?
Before I pour another drink, I'll look inside the glass.

Ultimate Betrayal

When my body let me down
it was the ultimate betrayal.
Once fit, and fast, and firm,
it's now fat, flabby, and frail.

It started with just a few
little aches and pains,
not serious enough
for me to complain.

When diagnosed, I learned
the word "autoimmune."
My body's defences
were attacking their own.

As each new symptom arrived
I discovered a repeating refrain:
the light deep in the tunnel
was often an oncoming train.

I've taken all of the pills,
and followed the doctors' advice.
Between disease and side effects,
the journey's not been very nice.

Now I'm stuck in this body
that never does what it ought.
I live with all the problems
this stupid disease has brought.

Please forgive me if I sometimes
complain too much about my strife.
I think I've earned the right to be
cheesed off with bits of my life.

Giving Up

I write about ghosts and monsters and things,
vampires take flight on leathery bat wings.
But the real-life monsters I fight again and again,
are the chronic illness struggles of exhaustion, and pain.

There are real horrors, too many people know,
like disease, poverty, war, and prejudice, so,
if I had a magic potion that wasn't just fictional,
I'd use it to end disease, poverty, war, hatred and all.

So that's what I'm thinking as I sit here in pain.
I've had bad days and I'm having one again.
I was meant to write a new chapter today,
but I'm sore and I'm sick and I can't concentrate.

So I'm giving up and going to bed.
I'll try to do better tomorrow.

Unhappy

I read on social media that:
"If you are unhappy,
you have three choices:
change the situation,
leave the situation,
or accept the situation."

Thank you for your advice,
well-meaning internet stranger.
Please let me tell you why,
your post inspired my anger.

I'm sometimes unhappy,
because I live with chronic pain.
Sometimes it eases a bit
then it gets worse again.

I can laugh and smile
on days of milder hurt,
but I get sad and irritable
when it's at its worst.

Think I change my situation?
Are you so far out of touch?
Medication and exercise help,
but they can only do so much.

Can I leave the situation?
Leave my body behind?
Surprisingly, there are people,
who would be sad if I died.

Perhaps I should accept my fate,
and put on a happy face.
I shouldn't let it bother me,
I should put it in its place.

But strangely, I am human,
and there's nothing I can do,
but handle it as best I can,
and still have feelings too.

Sometimes I will be sad,
and sometimes I'll be angry,
And that's a normal human way,
to handle my reality.

But supposing that my issue,
wasn't health, but injustice,
righteous anger's fuelled more reform
than happy denial ever did.

And what if what made me sad
was the horrible grief of loss,
Accepting takes a very long time
You can't rush the process.

Feelings are part of being human.
They're expressions of the soul.
We can't deny or destroy them.
They help to make us whole.

It is necessary to feel
the whole range of emotion.
Trying to suppress it
does not help anyone.

There are some emotions
that are seen as negative,
but we're only half human,
if we only feel positive.

It's impossible to stop
people feeling how we feel.
Better to accept emotions,
and learn how to deal.

Each person, as we grow,
and learn how to get along,
needs to learn how to handle
emotions when they're strong.

If seeing someone sad
makes you uncomfortable,
perhaps you should learn to cope,
instead of living in denial.

So sorry dear internet stranger,
I can't take your advice.
Even if living in your weird world
might seem very nice.

Walking Fanta

She's stubborn and strong
and she pulls me along.
As we go on our walk,
she says "bork bork"
to the dogs that we meet
as we walk down the street.
I tell her, "Be quiet,"
but she'd rather a riot.
She can't be tamed,
too stubborn to train.
We've worked hard at it,
but training never sticks.
She pretends to forget,
but I rather bet,
she knows right from wrong,
and just strings me along.
She's stronger than me,
powerful doggy,
and despite getting old,
she still won't be told.
She gives a devious grin,
with each doggy sin.
I'll go to my grave,
knowing she chose not to behave,
that she chooses if, where, and when,
she follows her training, sometimes, now and then.
Why do I love this exasperating fiend?
I know she loves me, right to the end.

Why

Why is the sky so blue, mother,
and why is it up so far away?
Blue's the colour of distance, child,
and the clouds need room to play.

Why is the grass so green, mother,
and why do the flowers have to die?
Green's the colour of growth, child,
and seeds help flowers return to life.

Why is the rock so brown, mother,
and why is the mountain so high?
Brown's the colour of strength, child,
and the mountain loves the sky.

Why is the night sky black, mother,
and why must we have night?
Black's the colour of darkness, child,
so the stars can twinkle bright.

Be Kind

The choice of good or evil
is never won and done.
It continues daily
in the heart of every one.

It's a daily balance,
and there's one basic tool,
Love's the central factor,
'though some want detailed rules.

Rules are fine as guidelines,
to judge actions of our own,
but when used for judging others,
can turn our hearts to stone.

A heart that's hard and cold,
will judge a neighbour, out of hand.
But a heart that's warm and loving,
will seek to understand.

If you want some advice
to ease your troubled mind,
whenever there's a choice,
just choose to be kind.

Earth

We live on a tiny ball
spinning its way through space.
It's the only one we know
can support the human race.

While we may one day find another
that possibly could suit,
if we don't survive until then,
the search would just be moot.

This ball of ours is precious.
It's the only one we have.
We've damaged it far to much,
but it's worth trying to save.

We can't take our home for granted,
in the way that we have been.
It's time to think about keeping
our ground, air, and water clean.

Sleep

I'm lying in bed
with a cat on my head
and the dog by my side
has gotten quite wide.

I'm trying to sleep
but the company I keep
feels more secure
when closer than near.

I could give them a shove,
but I accept their love
and submit to my fate,
I'll get to sleep late.

Eventually I doze,
And what do you know?
It's hyper coloured dreams,
on a weird range of themes.

The cat's growing a garden
of mutated flowers
while the dog talks philosophy
for hours and hours.

I think as I dream
therefore I'm confused
as the monsters arrive
of course, mermaids too.

For a moment I wake:
the cat yowls for yowl's sake.
The dog moves around,
takes the blankets, that hound.

I drift off again,
I guess that is when
the dreams all turn bad
and nightmares are had.

*The monsters are back
and there are more.
I don't want to count,
but at least a score.*

*Out of the garden
the cat's weird flowers
have begun to develop
strange magical powers.*

*The monsters and flowers
are chasing me down.
Somehow they think
I'd stole the Queen's crown.*

*But the Queen is dead
I'd read on the news.
I seek help from the dog
but she just quotes Rousseau.*

*The cat doesn't care
what her garden has done.
I have no help
I just have to run.*

*The flowers are gaining.
The monsters are, too.
I've run out of strength,
I think that I'm through.*

Then I hear a musical shriek.
As the alarm wakes me from sleep.
It's time to wake, the day's new
as for the pets, they both want food.

Anzac Day

On Anzac Day we're urged to remember
those who died as a price of war,
but spare a thought for those who came back,
and continue to pay more and more.

At the tomb of a soldier unknown
remember the known one too.
The one disabled, the one in the psych ward,
the street-dweller begging from you.

War brings death, we remember,
when the Anzac history's spoken.
But please remember, not just the dead,
but those who came back broken.

They were all young once,
with goals and hopes and dreams,
They went where they were ordered,
no questioning what orders mean.

The people who choose what wars to fight
are never on the front line.
They play with lives and futures
and act like that is fine.

War should be a last resort,
only when all else has failed.
A country's youth is not a resource,
that should be cheaply for sale.

Surely lives ought not be forsaken
to buy vague political points.
Sending young people to fight should be
only done when there's no other choice.

People Watching

The shopping centre was crowded.
A wall of noise overwhelmed me.
It's the nature of big places like that.
They're just too people-y.

So I sought the quiet,
of a cute little coffee shop.
With chocolate cake and a coffee,
I waited for the anxiety to stop.

In this quiet place,
where things were not so loud,
I saw individual people,
not just an anonymous crowd.

A child in a sports uniform,
having arvo tea with his Dad,
was glowing and animated,
telling about the game he had.

In the corner two advanced-aged teens
were giggling about days long before
with American soldiers based here
while "our boys" were off fighting a war.

On the other side of the room,
a woman seemed set for the duration,
as if belting away on her laptop
would save the life of a nation.

As the kid told how he scored that goal,
his voice was an excited squeak.
The Dad was quiet, and attentive,
listening to his child speak.

The girls in the corner had exciting jobs
they hadn't been allowed to before,
and were enjoying dances most nights.
Who said nobody wins in a war?

Laptop woman had finished her coffee
and asked for another brew.
Whatever she was frantically writing,
she was determined to power on through.

The Dad said he was proud of the kid
for doing his best at the game.
Even if the kid's team had lost,
he'd still be proud, all the same.

The former teens were on ration books,
and drawing fake seams on their legs.
Oh the wonders they used to bake
despite the shortage of flour and eggs.

While guzzling coffee, computer woman,
continued typing for Australia,
but slammed the laptop in disgust,
when the battery finally failed her.

And then my coffee was all gone,
bill paid, plate taken away.
It was time to face the noisy crowd,
and go once more into the fray.

Pizza

It's hot and it's fresh.
It's ready to please.
With spicy salami
and hot gooey cheese.

A small touch of basil,
oregano and chives.
A warm bread base,
the taste comes alive.

Rich red tomato sauce
adds a flavour hit.
You know once we start,
we won't stop eating it.

A yeasty, cheesy smell,
aroma of herb and spice.
You put on the movie.
I'll get us each a slice.

Money

They say money can't buy happiness
to some extent that's true.
But money would be handy
when all the bills come due.

Living on the financial edge,
or struggling on even less,
and budgeting with nothing,
creates a lot of stress.

I'm sure there comes a point
when more cash will not help,
when unexpected costs are easy
when bills don't cause a yelp.

But that point is limited
to the very privileged few.
A few more bucks still matter
to the likes of me and you.

They say money can't buy happiness.
I'd like to put it to the test.
Give me millions of dollars.
See if I'm at my happiest.

Oh the things I'd love to buy,
like a home with disabled access.
I'd pay my bills with a smile,
and use the hashtag "Truly blessed."

I'd help the people I know
who've struggled just like me.
Hashtag: "blessed to be a blessing."
I could give generously.

But as it is I must struggle
with expenses day to day,
trying my best to budget for
all the bills I'll need to pay.

I still find my happiness
how, when, and where, I can
but paying each expense
requires a careful plan.

I spend far too much energy
on paying for day to day stuff.
I don't really need millions,
I'd be happy with enough.

As the cost of living rises
there's more and more like me.
We don't really need a huge amount,
just enough to be happy.

Bees

Won't someone think of the bees?
That pollinate flowers and trees,
with pollen up to their knees.
Oh think of the bees, please.

Why not grow them some flowers?
You could keep them happy for hours.
Little bees work hard for our good,
and help plants supply our food.

Don't waste space with boring old lawn
and leave hungry bees all forlorn.
Plant some flowers, maybe some fruit.
You know the bees will think it's beaut.

If you want your fruit and veggies,
not to forget sweet, sweet, honey,
then our little friends must fly free.
Won't someone think of the bees?

Time

Sixty seconds to a minute.
Tick tock tick tock.
Sixty minutes to an hour.
Tick tock tick tock.

Time's regular and measured,
but it doesn't seem that way.
My children are adults.
They were babies yesterday.

Twenty-four hours to a day.
Tick tock tick tock.
Seven days to a week.
Tick tock tick tock.

I don't even know
how I got this old.
There's still so much to do,
so many stories to be told

Three hundred and sixty-five days to a year.
Tick tock tick tock.
Ten years to a decade.
Tick tock tick tock.

Illness made me set
so many dreams aside.
Can I achieve the rest?
Will I have the time?

Tick tock tick tock tick

To be a Better Person

I'd try to be less judgemental, but
that truckie is insane.
What idiot doesn't check their mirror
before a change of lane?

I'd try to be less gluttonous, but
there's ice-cream in the freezer,
and I know how to make cake.
Indulging is far too easy.

I'd try to stop procrastinating, but
how much time will that take?
I'll just read a little bit longer.
I'll deal with other stuff later.

I'd try to be more organised, but
I forgot I already had plans.
I made a vague note about it,
that I no longer understand.

I'd try to be more tidy, but
I just create a mess.
I don't remember where things go,
I can't even guess.

I'd try to be more positive, but
let's just try to get real.
Why smile and look happy,
if it's not really how I feel?

I'd try to be a better person,
if it weren't so hard a task.
Perhaps I could cover my failings,
and wear a fancy mask.

Or otherwise, I could try
to do things another way.
I could accept myself as I am,
and just be myself today.

Walk

Our walks are slower now, old friend.
I must apologise to you.
I know that you would love to run,
If only I could too.

You love to sniff your favourite spots,
as we shuffle along together.
You assume people we see,
will just love you for ever.

When you succeed at getting
a stranger to give you a pat,
you wear that doofy doggy grin
the whole way there and back.

Sometimes we miss a day or two,
sometimes a week or more.
But you're excited when I'm able,
and we head out the front door.

You encourage me to move
no matter how unwell I feel.
It's so very hard to refuse
a dog with excited zeal!

Coffee

Coffee makes me happy,
picks me up when I'm tired.
My first cup in the morning,
helps me be inspired.

When the day is overwhelming,
coffee always understands.
And when the weather's cold,
The full mug warms my hands.

I drink that first cup black,
and it helps me to wake.
Later mocha or cappuccino,
is for variation's sake.

I praise whoever first found,
this truly magic bean.
Could I be addicted
to glorious caffeine?

Happy Birthday

Happy birthday to me,
I feel a hundred and three.
Mid-fifties feel old
when lupus takes hold,
I'd love a day pain-free.

Happy birthday once more,
I feel ancient and sore.
All my joints ache,
and the pills that I take
I'm swallowing by the score.

Happy birthday, guess what?
I'm complaining a lot,
but really I'm glad,
with the life I've had,
there's still so much I've got.

I've a great family
and love flowing free,
I've a reason to live,
and still much to give,
and so happy birthday to me.

I'd Like to be a Cat

Oh to be a fluffy feline,
and nap throughout the day.
There'd never be any work to do,
just eat and sleep and play.

Sometimes people worry
about getting old or fat.
But there's no need to worry,
if you're a fluffy cat.

A kind servant would brush my hair,
check my food supply was fine.
They'd run whenever I meowed,
if I were a cute feline.

I would flop in a dishevelled heap,
and they'd still say I was cute.
I could be adorable,
stealing laces from a boot.

There's no expectation of a cat,
except to just exist,
and the purpose of a human
is to serve a kitty-kit.

Sleepless

trying to sleep
wakefulness
watchfulness
thoughts
turning
burning
churning
sleep a distant dream
what if
castles in clouds
unlikely futures
wisps of possibility
thoughts creep
prevent sleep
brain buzzed with fatigue
thoughts go on and on and on
ambling
rambling
shambling
thoughts won't turn off
won't stop
even newborn babies know how to sleep
how could I forget something so basic

April

It's April, in the midst of autumn.
The roses burst into glorious bloom.

Bright colours fill the garden,
air carries delicate scent.

The summer heat finally fades,
cool nights for rest are made.

Lengthening nights, shortening days,
milder weather should stop and stay.

Time to recover from summer burn.
Prepare for cold, which comes in turn.

Adventures in Brain Fog

The day I lost my mind
was like any other day.
Except my thoughts just wandered,
and then they stayed away.

Now my short-term memory
isn't what it ought…
I don't know what I was saying
I guess I just forgot.

Sometimes I lose focus,
and thinking's a hard slog.
It's cognitive dysfunction,
or commonly, brain fog.

My thoughts and memories
are somewhere in the mist.
If there's things I must remember,
I'll have to write them on a list.

I have to write a note,
If I have something to do,
Otherwise I'll forget,
where, when or with who.

At times my mind visits,
comes back from holiday.
I try to make the most of it.
I've learned it won't stay.

So I write when I'm able
and do whatever else I can too,
because when my mind goes fuzzy,
there's not much I can do.

Here's to cognitive dysfunction.
Why am I in the kitchen now?
Did I take my pills today?
I guess, I'll get by, somehow.

To My Younger Self

Life is hard right now, and it will get harder,
but the road's not at an end, you'll go much farther.
You have been told you are weak and a fool,
no-one can care about someone like you,
no-one could care, or value your heart,
but really you are strong, resilient, and smart.
Right now you feel you are broken,
and can't remember a kind word spoken.
Those critical voices of the past will never leave
but, with work, you will learn to make them behave.
You can learn to recognise the lies you're sold
understand you are not what you've been told.
To make the future better than the past,
you need to learn to love yourself at last.
When you learn to meet some of your own needs,
not sacrifice yourself for others' greed,
you'll learn you are more capable than you know.
Given the chance, you'll grow and grow.
Your anxious life will finally find calm
when you free yourself of those who do you harm.
Eventually, you'll discover friends who are true,
who'll love you, just for being you.
But to leave this past and find that new,
the first person to love you must be you.

Another Day

As I try to fall asleep,
I pick apart the day.
The things I've got wrong,
the mistakes I've made.

I think what I ought've done
to avoid all going wrong.
How I always seem so weak
when I mean to be strong.

Then I think back days and years
 the times I've messed up.
The steps from embarrassed child
to insecure grown up.

If I am to sleep at all,
I must pack those thoughts away.
I know I cannot change the past.
Tomorrow's another day.

Old Toys

New toys bring happiness
and giggles of great joy
when they're newly given to
excited girls and boys.

But old toys have a story
the things that they can tell.
About the change and growth
of the person they know well.

The toy who kept you safe
from the monster under the bed,
listened to your tears when
that first romance was dead.

Maybe you felt silly packing them
when you moved from home,
but you couldn't leave them behind,
and face the adult world alone.

And whatever changed in life:
work, home, family, and age,
one friend was always there
when you started a new stage.

They may be almost forgotten
hidden, and stored away.
Or maybe your old friend
is very proudly on display.

Either way, you know
the history you share,
whenever you need them,
your old friend's always there.

Your friend carries your secrets
and knows you through and through.
You know they're just a toy
because they're also part of you.

Maybe your old friend
fell apart along the way,
broke beyond repair
but in your heart they stay.

Another Earth

Suppose we found another Earth
somewhere out in space.
Would we care for it better
than we've done with this place?

Suppose it was all growing green
with blue and pristine, seas.
Could we minimise our impact
as we made it meet our needs?

Would we make the same mistakes?
Would just our presence sow the seed
of sacrificing the environment
to satiate human greed?

What if we learned some more respect
for the Earth we've already got in strife?
What if we learned to live in harmony
with the planet that gives us life?

There may not be another Earth
even beyond our Milky Way.
This place where we live right now,
may be the only place we stay.

And if we want to stay alive
on this planet we call home.
We need to change our wasteful ways
and try to fix what we have done

Clouds

Troubles gather like clouds
From nowhere
Slowly at first
Building up
Darkening the sky
Coming faster
Ominous
Threatening
Dangerous

A friend
Who listens
Who hears
Who understands
Helps find solutions
Interrupts the storm
Sunlight through the clouds.

Fairy Dust

A sprinkle of fairy dust
sparkling bright
glimmers and glitters
and brightens the night.

The forgotten joys
of childhood long gone,
memories of laughter
memories of song.

When life's at its darkest,
when gloom's over all,
it's hard to remember
there's joy to recall.

But that's when we need
some fairy dust most,
the times when we're sad,
the times when we're lost.

Adulthood is hard,
with the burdens we bear,
We need childish delight,
a bit, here and there.

Star

They left their home
for a country afar.
They watched the night sky
and followed a star.

They crossed barriers
of country and faith,
following a light,
in search of the great.

They went to a palace
in search of a king
not knowing the danger
that visit would bring.

The child-king they sought
had no privilege at all:
he made his home
among the most poor.

Some times what we seek
is not what we find.
Questions and answers
don't always align.

When a star calls you forth
into your own night,
perhaps you will find
an unexpected light.

Windmill

Soft breeze blows
Blades turn slowly
Metal groans quietly
Pump reaches down
Deep into arid earth
Treasure from aquifer
Water brings life
Life to cattle
Life to ground
Life to birds
Life to wildlife
Life to the outback

Tortise

You're eighty years old and still just middle aged,
you must have seen so much, across the world's stage.
Now you are so big most predators won't see you as food,
Life should be so easy, and everything so good.
But humans are strange predators, size no discouragement.
Sailors stopping at your island, left your population spent.
Your home really needed an ambassador such as you,
and you travelled across the world, to stay here at the zoo.
You help to raise awareness, while in the zoo you roam,
and if you have babies, you'll help repopulate your home.
Now your island is protected for tortoises, slow-paced,
There's no cause to fear now, no human hunters to race.

The Twelve Days of COVID

On the first day of COVID, the virus gave to me:
a nose running fairly freely.

On the second day of COVID, the virus gave to me:
two hacking coughs
and a nose running fairly freely.

On the third day of COVID, the virus gave to me:
three sneezes
two hacking coughs
and a nose running fairly freely.

On the fourth day of COVID, the virus gave to me:
four aching joints
three sneezes
two hacking coughs
and a nose running fairly freely.

On the fifth day of COVID, the virus gave to me:
five positive tests
four aching joints
three sneezes
two hacking coughs
and a nose running fairly freely.

On the sixth day of COVID, the virus gave to me:
six sleeping problems
five positive tests
four aching joints
three sneezes
two hacking coughs
and a nose running fairly freely.

On the seventh day of COVID, the virus gave to me:
seven bouts of brain fog
six sleeping problems
five positive tests
four aching joints
three sneezes
two hacking coughs
and a nose running fairly freely.

On the eighth day of COVID, the virus gave to me:
eight killer headaches
seven bouts of brain fog
six sleeping problems
five positive tests
four aching joints
three sneezes
two hacking coughs
and a nose running fairly freely.

On the ninth day of COVID, the virus gave to me:
nine antivirals
eight killer headaches
seven bouts of brain fog
six sleeping problems
five positive tests
four aching joints
three sneezes
two hacking coughs
and a nose running fairly freely.

On the tenth day of COVID, the virus gave to me:
ten scrambled tastebuds
nine antivirals
eight killer headaches
seven bouts of brain fog
six sleeping problems
five positive tests
four aching joints
three sneezes
two hacking coughs
and a nose running fairly freely.

On the eleventh day of COVID, the virus gave to me:
eleven fits of coughing
ten scrambled tastebuds
nine antivirals
eight killer headaches
seven bouts of brain fog
six sleeping problems
five positive tests
four aching joints
three sneezes
two hacking coughs
and a nose running fairly freely.

On the twelfth day of COVID, the virus gave to me:
twelve nights of fever
eleven fits of coughing
ten scrambled tastebuds
nine antivirals
eight killer headaches
seven bouts of brain fog
six sleeping problems
five positive tests
four aching joints
three sneezes
two hacking coughs
and a nose running fairly freely.

Bauble

A glass Christmas bauble, shiny and bright,
encircled by glitter, reflecting the light.
It hangs on the tree amid tinsel and lights,
a strange commemoration of such a strange night.

A young woman gave birth, homeless, in the gloom.
Her poor tradie husband couldn't find them a room.
The birth was attended by local working poor,
but announced by angels singing a heavenly score.

Later, faithful foreigners of another religion,
came to bring gifts, calling the baby a king.
But the rich and powerful of the day,
saw him as a threat to get out of the way.

The family had to flee their own country,
to take their infant and become refugees,
while the powerful at home tormented the poor,
and took from them the children they bore.

And strangely now we remember that night,
with snow-covered scenes, and glitter and lights,
we cover the pain, the danger and fear,
with fantasy Christmas cards, full of bright cheer.

And strangely we remember that tiny baby,
not by helping the poor, homeless, or refugee,
but by decorating the Christmas tree,
and displaying wrapped gifts for all to see.

A glass Christmas bauble, shiny and bright,
encircled by glitter, reflecting the light.
It hangs on the tree amid tinsel and lights,
a strange commemoration, for such a strange night.

Writer, Not Serial Killer

Don't annoy the author, let me tell you why:
I'll put you in a story, then I'll make you die.

I have no qualms in killing a fictional you.
So be careful what you say, and be careful what you do.

I could forgive. I could forget. But where's the fun in that?
When I could write some words, and make you go splat!

I could push you down a staircase, or stab you in the night.
I could write a horror story, and make you die of fright.

Revenge is fun in fiction, there's no limit to what I write.
Look out, the killer's following, while you walk alone at night.

Forget conventional revenge. I won't slander your name
around town,
You'll die in a dark alley, killed by a psychotic clown.

I'll put you in my story. You can read it through.
You may not even realise; only I'll know for sure it's you.

So don't annoy the author. While I write, don't bother me.
Or I'll put you in my story, and you'll die horribly!

Bubbles

A puff of breath,
trapped in a rainbow film,
floats on air,
on breeze to roam,
to float,
to fly,
a moment of wonder,
of whimsy.
Air floating on air,
shining, bright,
a thing of light.
To land and to burst:
detergent splotch.
Float no more,
wonder's lost.

Rose

A rose is a feast for the senses
the perfection of flowers.
It presents complete delight
for all the sensory powers.

The sight of a rose is art.
Each petal a lover's pledge.
The vivid colour subtly changes
from deep centre to pale edge.

The scent of the rose evokes memories.
Perfumes of loved people and places.
It transports us back through time,
and through so many different spaces.

The feel of the rose is delicate
when caressing a soft petal,
but the leaf is tough like leather
and the stem has spikes of metal.

The taste of the rose is exotic
rosewater dances over the tongue,
In cakes, and Turkish delight,
the taste is second to none.

The sound of the rose is silence,
gentle peace of the quiet garden.
Who doesn't crave that silent,
quiet, peace now and then?

You could give me a hundred cut roses,
and I would love them for a while.
But plant them in the garden,
and they'd always make me smile.

Afternoon Walk

You saw me limping down the path, leaning on my walking
stick.
Whatever lead you to decide to grab a boob real quick?

Was it excess weight, greying hair or disability
or just being a woman, that made you target me?

Perhaps it took you by surprise when I let out that scream,
and raised the stick to hit you, 'cause I'm tougher than I
seem.

I guess it was good luck for me, that you ran off down the
path.
I could have been arrested if it turned to a bloodbath.

Everyone has a story you don't know unless you're told.
This sick middle-aged woman, wasn't always sick or old.

Lupus damaged my body; wrecked it, in fact, in parts,
but part of me remembers when I was good at martial arts.

Somewhere in my mind I hear a long-past coach's voice:
Don't stop to think, just act. There's no time for a choice.

And on this day I acted without stopping for a thought.
And, startled, you just ran away, exactly as you ought.

Here's a message to the creeps who think women are just
prey:
some of us are angry now, and you won't have your way.

Time Doesn't Heal

They say time heals all wounds
but that's really not the truth.
It's a well-intentioned, but
ultimately cruel, myth.

When we first hear the awful news
someone we love is lost,
we find ourselves faced with
an unbelieving shock.

When shock dissipates,
we are left with unbearable pain.
Every thought, and every word,
brings the pain back again.

When the pain is older
we start to get the chance,
to put things in perspective,
and begin the emotional dance.

We move from grief to anger,
to depression and back to pain.
We dance from one feeling to another,
and dance our way back again.

It seems to be unending
as we bounce to and fro.
Until the avalanche of emotion
finally begins to slow.

This is what time does for us,
though hard to see when grief is new,
it gives us a chance to learn
to live with loss we can't undo.

The pain will always be there,
though not harsh as at first.
We learn to savour memories
when grief's no longer at its worst.

As time moves on and more of life
follows on after what we've lost,
the tinge of sadness never goes,
but love's what we remember most.

Deep within our hidden hearts,
the pain of loss can't remove,
the joy and happiness we felt,
the reasons why we loved.

There can be joy again
though loss can't be undone.
There can be peace and hope,
there's even a chance for fun!

Time doesn't heal all wounds,
but it does give us the space,
to reflect and to move forward,
and let love take grief's place.

And while our memories
will be sad as well as sweet,
we can trust to love to hold us close
until we once more meet.

Dear Mum and Dad

Dear Mum and Dad,
from your daughter who's stuck.
I hate boarding school.
It's really just ... unbearably terrible.

There's a nasty teacher,
in a class I can't switch,
at least once each lesson,
she calls me a ... stupid child.

I got a new boyfriend.
He's already an ex.
I was uncomfortable
when he asked me ... to buy him stuff.

Then there's the class bully
who thinks she's just it.
She's really so cruel
she's just not worth ... my time or attention.

Please let me come home!
You know that you should!
I promise, I promise,
I've learned to be good.

The principal's crazy.
When I see him I run.
He patrols the halls
with a pen and a ... detention list.

My room mate just pulled
a horrible stunt.
She ripped up my homework.
She's just a ... truly horrible person.

The food's really awful.
The best bit's stale bread.
If I keep eating it
I know I'll end up ... with gastrointestinal upset.

The air conditioners broke
and the fans did as well.
Outside's forty degrees.
Inside it's hot as ... the surface of the planet Mercury.

Please let me come home!
Oh tell me you've heard!
If you let me come home,
I won't use "bad words".

Journey

Life is a journey, so I've heard,
but no-one said which way to turn.
So many choices, so much stress!
I didn't get my map or GPS!

Forward or back or here or there.
Am I getting someplace, or going nowhere?
There's choices to make each day, week and year,
and consequences aren't always so clear.

Keep in balance, health, time, and money,
Make a mistake and it's not funny.
Family and work, hobbies and rest,
balance them out or there's a mess.

If I could backtrack to a time long ago
when some big choices set the way I would go,
if the consequences of what I'd chosen were clear
who would I become, now and here?

But there's no going back, no u-turns allowed,
I'm right where I am, and there's no backing out.
The many choices which got me to here,
should have been lessens, but they weren't so clear.

So when the new choices are present today,
"What could go wrong?" I hear myself say.
"What could go wrong?" I think of the past.
I stop to consider. I'm learning at last.

What can go wrong probably will;
often at the worst time possible.
That being said, it's a fact of life,
I have to keep going whatever the strife.

When I look at the choices that come day by day,
I think of the risks and I hope and I pray.
I hope for the path of the overall best,
there's no going back to try the rest.

Maybe I'll regret the paths I don't take,
but since it's my journey, it's not a mistake.
Whatever I've done, wherever I've been,
it's all my journey though the map's unseen.

I hope when the journey finally ends,
I'll at last see that map and it will make sense.
Choices that seemed bad and those that seemed good,
will all come together, just as they should.

Whether smooth highways, back alleys or rough tracks,
I hope the wrong turns will eventually lead back,
to the road I'd have followed if I'd had GPS,
to a life that was good, well-lived, more or less.

Dust

"Dust you are and to dust you will return."

I am dust.
I am carbon and hydrogen and oxygen
and iron and calcium and nitrogen and phosphorus.
I am the stuff of soil and rock,
of plants and trees and animals,
of water and air.
I am the stuff of stars and planets.
I am the stuff of coral reefs and ocean depths.
I am the stuff of creeks and forests.
I am the stuff of clouds and wind and rain.

I am a part of the whole of creation.
What is good for earth and air and water
and plants and animals
is good for me.
What harms earth and air and water
and plants and animals
harms me.
I must tread softly on this earth,
for it is me and I am it,
and you and me are we,
and we are part of all that lives.
We are dust
and to dust we will return.
The earth feeds us
and nurtures us.
We will feed the soil,
and nurture the earth.
People and planet
must grow and work together,
because we are all dust.

Wishing Well

Make a wish and throw a coin
into the wishing well.
Will your wishes come true?
Only time can tell.

Will you wish to help a friend?
Will you wish for wars to end?
Will you wish for cash to spend?
Will you wish a rift to mend?

Just a coin to gain access
to the magic built on hope.
Hope is magic for the times,
you don't know how to cope.

Will you wish for a new pet?
Will you wish to own a jet?
Will you wish to win a bet?
Will you wish your needs were met?

We all want to change the world,
to wish it were different, somehow.
Sometimes we want to change the past.
Sometimes we want to change the now.

Will you wish to learn some truth?
Will you wish to regain youth?
Will you wish back a lost tooth?
Will you wish you weren't uncouth?

A coin thrown in a wishing well
changes nothing real.
But reflecting on your wishes
can change how you feel.

Will you wish to change your life?
Will you wish an end to strife?
Will you wish to make things right?
Will you wish troubles weren't rife?

A wish can grow into intent
to change what's gone astray.
Intent can grow into a plan,
and you're on your way.

Mushrooms

Wild mushrooms will appear
in the damp earth after rain.
They might be gone for ages,
when it's rained they're back again.

If you step on a mushroom
you may hear a satisfying pop,
might see fungal explosion,
and see no reason to stop.

Don't step on that mushroom
that grew up in your lawn.
It could just be a fungus
it could be someone's home.

You're too old for magic
so now you might not see
that mushroom could be a house
for pixies or queen fairy.

Now you may laugh and say
that it's just preposterous.
Remember you were a child
who trusted this truth once.

When it's rained and mushrooms
grow wild from the damp ground
recall the child you used to be,
and keep magic around.

Vampire's Kiss

Awaking from a fevered dream,
a memory of mesmerising eyes,
a voice, low and strong fading into the night.
Lethargy. Overwhelming fatigue.
Two small wounds on pale skin,
so much paler than before.
Blood smear on the pillow.
Confusion. A sense of dread desire
for something unknown.
A window left open to the night.
A sense of something demanded,
something taken,
nothing given in return.
A kiss that always takes and never gives.
He will be back tomorrow.
His kiss will bring her death.

Fragile

You knew my heart was fragile
yet you broke it.
You knew the word would hurt
yet you spoke it.

All that I ever had
you just took it.
I sent you all my love
you forsook it.

Now, though bent and broken
I carry on.
I am so much stronger
now you are gone.

Nice Guy

He was a Nice Guy
so the bruises when they were showed,
were tiny, just fingerprints.
A Nice Guy would never hit a woman,
so he just yelled at unexpected times
and grabbed her very hard instead.

He was a Nice Guy
so when she complained
he would buy her presents.
He gave her flowers
or things he wanted for himself
but gave to her,
so she had to be grateful
(if she knew what was good for her).

He was a Nice Guy
so when she cowered in fear
and did everything she could to avoid him,
he absolutely knew she was having an affair
because there was no other possible reason
any woman could resist
a Nice Guy like him.

He was a Nice Guy
who would lock her possessions
away in the shed.
When she said she wanted things back
he would tell her she could go and get them,
but he would never, ever,
tell her where he hid the key.

He was a Nice Guy
and he made sure everyone around her
saw what a Nice Guy he was,
and how much he did for her.
So when she looked for help or support,
people told her how lucky she was
to have such a Nice Guy as him.

He was a Nice Guy
and Nice Guys deserve a little something
for being so very, very Nice.
So he spent all her money,
ran up bills she couldn't pay,
and explained to her how selfish she was
if she wanted anything at all for herself.

He was a Nice Guy
and he spoke on her behalf
saying what she thought and
what she wanted
since he was so Nice he knew what
she ought to think and feel and believe
and she shouldn't have to
do that for herself.

He was a Nice Guy
and she lived in fear
but when she saw her children afraid
she finally found her strength.
She lost everything except them
when she started over again.
She swore to herself,
she'd never fall
for such a Nice Guy again.

He was a Nice Guy
and when she finally left
everyone rallied around
to support him.
Because she was so very cruel
to abandon
such a Nice Guy as him.

Happy and Free

Wanda the whale
wandered the sea.
A whale's life
is happy and free.

Wanda would swim
Wanda would sing
She had no care
about anything.

A gigantic beast,
smaller beasts on board,
followed her a while,
and made her scared.

The beast was so loud,
she was disturbed,
Her lovely whale song
couldn't be heard.

She decided then
to avoid such beasts.
But as problems go,
it wasn't the least.

Swimming the Pacific
she stopped to stare
at an island of rubbish
that shouldn't be there.

Wander then wondered
about all that mess.
It was just wrong
and caused her distress.

Wanda the whale
still wandered the sea.
Because of humans,
no longer happy.

Rainbows and Unicorns

Rainbows and unicorns, faeries and gnomes,
there's a magical world, not far from home.

Down the garden path, in forest, near stream,
the magic is waiting, you know what I mean.

Feel the whimsy of a magical location,
there's always a way through imagination.

Whatever you're doing, wherever you are,
faeries and unicorns are never far.

Let's go for a walk, just down this path,
over the rainbow and on to the stars.

Let's dance with faeries and ride unicorns.
Forget being grownups this magical morn.

Wind

I whisper so low when I rustle the leaves
I tussle your hair as a soft, gentle breeze.

I raise your kite high, on a bright clear day.
But don't think you can tame me just 'cause I sometimes play

I bring sea air from the east, and raise dust in the west.
I howl through the night when you can't find your rest.

You ride me with sailboats, with hang gliders, too.
I'm welcome on hot days, when I am cool.

I turn the huge turbines which give you your power.
But you don't control me, not ever, not now.

I chop the sea waves, a cyclone, storm, or a squall.
Then I cross to the land, and I don't stop or stall.

I lift off your roof, and I knock down your walls.
Whatever you build, I can make it all fall.

You take me for granted, but give me my due,
You may often need me, but I'll never need you.

Turtle Song

You've swum the ocean currents
for sixty years or more.
Have you felt the oceans changing:
a bit warmer more than before?

On your way to lay your eggs,
back on your familiar beach,
did you see the difference?
Did you see the coral bleach?

Did you see the litter
that humans left behind.
Did you worry for your babies,
incubating in the sand?

Are the kelp forests still growing
the way they always did?
Are the fish as plentiful?
Are crabs and prawns and squid?

Have you seen floating plastic,
and thought "jellyfish"?
Have you swallowed something strange
which made you sick for a bit?

Have you gained some wisdom
as you've swum around the world?
Something you'd tell humans,
if you could speak the words?

We need to change our ways,
We know we really must.
If it's too late for you,
it could be too late for us.

The Edge

Everything important has an edge,
trust and truth, responsibility, legality, and morality.
Some are cautious and stay well back
while others forgo their safety.

Those who get closer to the edge,
will find that they can see:
the view is better, the risk is greater.
One jump and you are free.

You can live your life on the edge
and never take that jump.
Or you can leap and fly -
until the landing thump.

You can throw things from the edge,
values, truth, the money you own,
but when you follow them over,
what you've thrown will let you down.

There's no guardrail at the top
nor any safety net below.
The wise stay carefully back.
If they must approach, they're slow.

But the edge casts a magic spell
and not all can resist the call:
they cannot resist coming closer
until, inevitably, they fall.

Old Books Never Die

There's magic waiting
in op shops and second-hand stores.
Portals to adventure and mystery
to future and history.
Portals opened by others
but ready for use again,
ready to show you
what others have seen,
ready to take you
on the paths where they've been.
Step into a world
as fresh now as then.
Give life to a story
told once again.
Old books never die.
Their stories live for ever.

Red Sky, Black Sky

Lightning strikes tree
sparks burn brightly.

Animals run.
It's just begun.

Sparks light dry tree
fire spreads quickly

Red sky at night
bushfire's alight.

Eucalypt oil burns
fire roars, runs, turns.

Nature is life.
It's death tonight.

Black sky morning
fire's still burning.

Fire creates wind,
wind spreads fire again.

Unpredictable dragon
flame breath burns on.

Fight it or flee,
don't "wait and see."

Eucalypt forest
fire doesn't rest.

Runs down valley,
up hills, easily.

Wildlife is caught,
with death or hurt.

Fight it and choke
on eucalypt smoke.

Water bomb dropped
Chopper's aloft.

Firefighters below
won't let it grow.

Fire beast attacks,
firies fight back.

Smokey black pall
hangs over all.

Life in balance
is there a chance?

Muscles and sweat,
fighting still yet.

Dragon attacks,
then is fought back.

Firies fight on
til all flame is gone.

Forest is black.
Life will come back.

Koala

I eat and I pee
and I sleep in the tree.
I'm cute as can be.
You know you love me.

I'm fussy about
the trees where I live.
Food, water, and home,
my favourite trees give.

My habitat's shrinking
I'm now in decline,
You've taken my home.
What's now yours was mine.

You may ooh and aah
when you see me in a zoo.
But if you plant enough trees
I could still live free too.

Pay some attention
when you're out on a walk.
I grunt and I growl,
but I can't yell or talk.

But if I could speak
you know what I'd say.
I'm still here now,
and I'd like to stay.

So look up when you're out
and check all the trees.
Now could be your
last chance to see me.

Simple Pleasures

Life has simple pleasures
that never should get old,
sneaking ice cream before dinner,
and a favourite story told.

The swing you rode as a child
when you almost reached the sky,
is still fun if you ride it,
with greying hair and bleary eye.

A colouring book or a game,
made for someone under ten,
is also fun for grandparents
to enjoy now and then.

And who said plasticine,
poster paints, or paper mache
were only for the children
when adults want to play?

Adults' days get dreary,
when tied to the daily grind.
It's far too easy to forget
we also need to unwind.

Surrounded by work, and bills,
responsibilities, and strife,
don't forget to take time for
the simple pleasures of life!

Human

To be human
in this world is
to live
to love
and to (often unwillingly) let go.

Faith hopes for a world
where we are able
to live
to love
and to never let go.

Hello Twenty Twenty-three

Hello, and welcome, Twenty Twenty-three.
What kind of year do you think you'll be?

Twenty Twenty, Twenty-one, Twenty-two,
set expectations very low for you.

Your older siblings weren't all that great.
They brought disease, disasters, war and hate.

The world-wide pandemic was never fun,
And invading your neighbours shouldn't be done.

We're tired of floods and bushfires and such.
We wanted a break, we weren't asking much.

The divide's increasing between rich and poor,
the poor live in need while the rich demand more.

But now you're here, all fresh and new
What can the world expect from you?

Could you please bring compassion, less greed?
A chance for everyone to have what they need?

Could you give the planet a bit of a break?
Have corporations give back, not just take?

Could you send the misogynists back to their caves?
Think of the trauma that one thing could save.

The past Twenty Twenties have let us down.
Will things be different, now you're around?

Wouldn't you want to be "that year" if you could?
Be the year we look back on and say, "It was good."

The Week Before Christmas

It was a week before Christmas
and things weren't going well,
Santa's cost-cutting measures
were beginning to tell.

The reindeer were weak,
from inferior food,
Elves working overtime,
were in a horrible mood.

The elves formed a union.
Reindeer did the same.
They presented Santa,
their demands for change.

Santa said, "Wait,
I have to pay rent,
and money for materials
is already spent."

"Expenses are up
cost of living is high.
Christmas is coming,
crunch time is nigh!"

The elves answered first.
Their point was quite true:
paying for labour's
a business cost too.

Reindeer added a point
he couldn't deny:
they couldn't deliver
when too weak to fly.

So Santa was stuck
in the workshop alone
while elves and reindeer
picketed in the snow.

Santa finally turned to
the smartest person he knew.
Mrs Clause had the answer.
She knew what to do.

Santa wasn't any old boss,
he ruled the north pole.
The economy was his,
the printing press as well.

Quantitive easing
was the thing to do,
she said, "Print more money.
Men just don't have a clue."

So money was printed
and the elves were all paid.
The reindeer were fed,
so they could pull the sleigh.

Christmas was saved,
for this year at least.
But coming next year,
is the inflation beast.

Then and Now

"What doesn't kill you makes you stronger"
or so the old saying said.
Sometimes, what doesn't kill you
just makes you wish you were dead.

She'd always tried to be nice
concerned with how others felt.
She'd never been as concerned
with protecting herself.

She'd given and given and given
more and more and more.
She'd given with no return
and she never kept the score.

Then the day came at last,
when she had nothing more to give.
When she had nothing left,
and no-one cared how she would live.

When she was left with nothing,
and had to try to start again,
no-one wanted to know,
and she was dearly short of friends.

When she picked herself up
not knowing how she found the strength.
Suddenly there was someone
who needed her once again.

The story repeated over and over
leaving her with so much trauma.
Each time, she was more broken,
but there was no help for her.

Eventually, she realised
she would have to change her ways.
She had to carefully choose
the people who filled her days.

She learned to only give
what she could afford.
She learned how to say "no"
to those who wanted more.

As she became that bit stronger,
she was no longer alone.
Others who had been as broken
saw her as one of their own.

The broken banded together
to lend each other strength.
Each knowing others would be there
when they needed help again.

The trauma didn't make her strong.
It really made her weak.
She only found her strength inside
a safe community.

Her community enfolds her
and helps protect her heart.
And she helps protect the others
when their problems start.

Now she looks so confident,
She appears in control.
It's still a very thin veneer
over the harm in her soul.

She still cares and still gives
when others do need help.
But there are limits now
and she protects herself.

She enforces boundaries,
now she knows what they are
And when she also needs support,
she knows someone who will care.

Never ever will she again,
risk her everything,
For the sake of those
who don't give her anything.

She won't risk her safety
or give her security away,
She knows people take advantage
and loving words betray.

She's done with starting over
with losing everything.
She's still a gentle rose,
But her thorns have gained a sting.

Treat her with respect
after all that she's been through.
She's willing to walk away
and leave your problems with you.

She knows she's not responsible
for any mess you've made.
Consequences for your actions
are just yours to be paid.

She may help you if she's able,
but she now knows her limits.
And she's more than willing to accept
her life without you in it.

Don't think you can control her
with threats to walk away.
She's learned to keep herself safe,
and won't beg you to stay.

Don't bother playing silly games.
She'll never play along.
She may have been a victim then,
but now she knows how to be strong.

Lupus Bites

Days of fatigue
nights full of pain
Lupus is snarling
as she slinks back again.

I live with the wolf,
she says in my ear,
Your life is now mine,
I'll always be here.

She takes such delight
in tormenting her prey
and oh what surprises
she brings day by day.

My mind often wanders.
It's slow to return,
I'm weak and I'm sore
my inflamed joints burn.

Her foul breath on my skin
brings fever and rash,
Too sick now for work,
life plans fall to ash.

She leaves me alone
just prowls for a while,
Suddenly, she attacks
with a bloody-fanged smile.

She'll kill me one day.
She's taken others I know.
That monstrous wolf bitch,
chooses when we will go.

But, like all other lupies,
I shout with hoarse voice:
"I'll keep fighting the wolf,
(because I have no choice.)"

I fight her with pills,
with diet, with rest.
I fight when I can,
and I hope for the best.

The fight leaves me drained,
so in painsomniac nights
I lie awake thinking
how much lupus bites.

Held Up in Transit

My world came crashing down, the day my coffee maker died.
I spent a day in shock, and periodically, I cried.

Then the answer came to me, just before the day was done.
I couldn't live without good coffee, so I'd buy another one.

I didn't have the cash. I did the only thing I could.
I put the thing on credit, even though I never should.

I ordered a really good one, it was on sale online,
I waited for a week. They really took their time.

(There'd been one in store in Oxley, less than an hour away.
I'd chosen "delivery", hoping it would come next day.)

Then I emailed the supplier, to ask when it would come,
I didn't get an answer, my anxiety did run.

Four more days later, I again went to their site,
I told the chat bot my story, and asked "Is this right?"

The bot put on a human who said, "I know I can fix this.
It will be just a few more days. You'll get it, I promise."

I got the tracking number, and I've got a story for ya:
instead of here in Queensland, it was coming from Victoria!

I watched the tracking page, for my coffee maker's journey,
it spent a night in Melbourne, then was on its way to me.

It only took a day to get to New South Wales.
If it kept going at that speed, there'd be no need for this tale.

Apparently New South was just the place to be,
It had a little holiday, at the depot in Botany.

Eventually, it moved again, I was relieved to see,
It was at Brisbane airport, so very close to me!

Next day I saw it listed as "on board for delivery,"
I waited all the day, but no package came for me.

Then I checked the tracking details. My emotions took a hit.
It was stuck at Woolloongabba, and "held up in transit."

Now I'm sniffing coffee beans, that I can't turn into a brew,
I'm desperately craving coffee, and I'm very grumpy too.

Here's the moral of my story, before I end my rant,
I never, ever, will again, take good coffee for granted.

I thought you'd like an update, to my extended story.
It took three more days to get here, but now the coffee's
flowing free.

Three weeks from when I ordered, early on Saturday,
I was woken by the message, it's been delivered to my place.

I rushed to my front door, and found a box marked "heavy".
I struggled to bring it in, but for coffee I was ready.

Unpacking it was awkward. Appliance boxes always are.
I nearly dropped it on the dog, before I got it free at last.

Here's advice to fellow addicts, if you're ever stuck like me,
I should've ordered "pick up", and just driven to Oxley.

Thoughts in an Old Cemetery

I walk between neglected plots
the soil now housing the dead,
As I note the names, the stories and dates,
Odd thoughts appear in my head.

A metre by two and another two down,
Is their final, their permanent, home,
Whatever in life they thought they had,
this is all they can now claim to own.

Ancient woman, near young farmer
near housewife, tradesman, and child.
Another child, another and another
before vaccines, disease ran wild.

Here they all are, forgotten by family
by descendants, by the town.
No longer tended, nor needed.
None remembered, or of any renown.

The giant monument stands
beside the modest headstone
stands by the unmarked grave
beside another and another one.

I wonder what difference it made,
the size of that memorial stone,
in your century below the soil,
where you lay all alone?

Did your family think they loved you more,
than all of your neighbours around?
Did they hope to buy you heaven?
Or status in this charnel ground?

Death's a leveller, so they say,
but here in the old cemetery.
It's still clear who had the money,
and whose death had to be free.

Now the mourners have left
the flowers long gone,
Great monument long forgotten,
just like the small stone.

The town bustles by too busy
to notice the old cemetery
Here we are left by ourselves
the stones and soil, the dead and me.

History

How will history remember our times?
How will our story be told?
Will it recall how people lost their minds
and hoarded toilet paper like a dragon's gold?

Will tomorrow's people understand
the fear of those who were vulnerable,
who were weak or sick or old,
when life seemed so unstable?

Will they then look back at us
and wonder how we survived
when so many argued for freedom
from the attempts to keep all alive?

Will they recall how much we needed
delivery drivers, supermarket staff, and nurses.
How we called them all our heroes,
But put no more pay in their purses.

We lurched from historic bushfires,
to global pandemic then devastating floods.
Now there's a new war in Europe,
The news just never seems good.

Through it all, some have looked out
for others around them in need.
While some have looked out for themselves
 and sought to feed their own greed.

In just a couple of years,
we've lived a dozen nightmares.
Will history judge us as selfish,
or will it see how much we can care?

The Stranger in the Mirror

I don't know this woman's face.
but she's in my mirror again
the swelling, rashes and scars
tell the story of her long-term pain.

These hands that are stiff
with joints that won't bend,
are clumsy and swollen
as they grasp at the pen.

Hips and knees that won't work,
a gut that's disturbed,
a brain always fuzzy,
and clumsy with words.

This woman's a stranger,
someone unfamiliar,
But lupus has made her
the one in my mirror.

Even now I still look
for the face I once knew.
before all this disease
has put me through.

Pollie Ticks

the pollies are ticking
tick tick tick
money from big business
tick tick tick
listen to lobbyists
tick tick tick
ignore the climate
tick tick tick
flood, fires and more flood
tick tick tick
scapegoat the vulnerable
tick tick tick
create fake issues
tick tick tick
cruelty to refugees
tick tick tick
ignore indigenous
tick tick tick
ignore all women
tick tick tick
assault accusations
tick tick tick
living cost rising
tick tick tick
too slow with vaccines
tick tick tick
weird publicity stunts
tick tick tick
PM makes a curry
tick tick tick
blame previous government
tick tick tick
welfare for the rich
tick tick tick
condemning the poor

tick tick tick
economy comes first
tick tick tick
so humans come last
tick tick tick
politics as usual
tick tick tick
the devil you know
tick tick BOOM!

Why It Matters

There's a post that's going around
Which purports to explain
why it really matters
to protect Ukraine.

Why Ukraine matters
according to the post
is all the rich resources,
the ore and grain and coal.

Ukraine really matters
for all it can provide.
So the shared post tells us,
but there's another side.

Ukraine matters in the
way all other nations do.
It's a country made of people
the same as me and you.

Ask a mother in Kyiv
what matters most to her.
It's keeping her family safe,
from the oncoming war.

While the tanks are rolling in
and death falls from the sky
we watch it on tv
and it matters to us, why?

It's not about the coal,
uranium, cheese or grain,
it's because deep down underneath
humans are all the same.

If we really do believe,
we deserve to live at peace,
we must believe that people there
deserve the same at least.

Human beings have value,
beyond all commodities.
You cannot put a price
on living safe and free.

While kids hide from missiles,
while families try to flee,
it's people who need compassion,
not the economy.

Winter's Tale

I want to stay in bed today,
the morning's way too cold.
The aches and pains are telling me
my body's getting old.

Autumn went by so very fast
and winter's taking hold.
A rainy, dismal winter,
now my house is full of mould.

There's a possum in my ceiling.
It moved in to get warm.
It made a hole to see that
I won't do it any harm.

If you ask me how I like the cold,
You know I'll tell you straight:
I'd rather stay in bed all day
and learn to hibernate.

The possum and the mould
could both be left to sit,
until springtime comes around
and I'd deal with all of it.

But humans, alas, are not
built to hibernate.
So cold winter mornings just
continue to draw my hate.

Lifters and Leaners

The phrase "lifters and leaners", divides the bad from good,
but who does the heavy lifting and who just leans on whom?

Who provides the labour that makes the economy turn?
And who rakes in the profits, those labourers have earned?

Who helps lift the poor, out of their poverty?
And who just condemns them for their lack of property?

Who would lift the sick, and help them back to health?
And who would let them die, if they can't pay the bill
themselves?

Who would help the depressed feel just a bit less glum?
And who cares about the harried, struggling single mum?

And who would lift the disabled, and help them on their way,
and help to make a safe space, for them to work and play?

Who lifts those who are different, in thought and in
appearance?
Who believes that everyone deserves to have a decent
chance?

Who will lift an old person who's fallen on the floor?
Who will help someone who's hungry, and needs just a little
more?

Who always does their very best, to help all those around
while they find their own problems still always abound?

Who pays all their taxes, hoping to help all those in need,
before that is diverted to subsidise the rich's greed?

Who leans on the poor, who are desperate for work,
and then pays them unfairly, because they're such a jerk?

Who leans on accumulated wealth so they don't have a care,
then minimises taxes so they don't pay their fair share?

Who looks down on the poor, and says they just don't "have a go,"
when they got their own start with inherited dough?

Who leans on the planet, to take all that it can give,
and cares so very little, to leave what we need to live?

Who leans on tired theories, like a "trickle down" economy,
then plugs up tiny leaks and says, "But this is just for me"?

The lifters do their best to help the sick, and frail, and poor,
While the leaners, lean on all of those and yet they still want more.

While lifters do their best to fight for fair conditions,
Wealthy leaners can just buy favourable politicians.

When politicians moan, please ask them what they mean
when they talk of those who lift and those who merely lean.

www.ingramcontent.com/pod-product-compliance
Lightning Source LLC
Chambersburg PA
CBHW071839090426

42737CB00012B/2301